# WAKA TAUA
## THE MAORI WAR CANOE

Also by Jeff Evans:

*Ngā Waka o Neherā*
*Polynesian Navigation and the Discovery of New Zealand*
*Notes on the Art of War* (Editor)
*Maori Weapons*

# WAKA TAUA
## THE MAORI WAR CANOE

## JEFF EVANS

Published by Oratia Books, Oratia Media Ltd, 783 West Coast Road,
Oratia, Auckland 0604, New Zealand (www.oratia.co.nz).

Copyright © 2000, 2017 Jeff Evans
Copyright © 2017 Oratia Books (published work)

The copyright holders assert their moral rights in the work.

This book is copyright. Except for the purposes of fair reviewing, no part of this publication may be reproduced or transmitted in any form or by any means, whether electronic, digital or mechanical, including photocopying, recording, any digital or computerised format, or any information storage and retrieval system, including by any means via the Internet, without permission in writing from the publisher. Infringers of copyright render themselves liable to prosecution.

ISBN 978-0-947506-39-1

First published 2000 by Reed Books (NZ)
Reprinted 2005
Second edition 2013 by Libro International
Reprinted 2014
This edition 2017 by Oratia Books

Printed in New Zealand

# Contents

| | |
|---|---|
| Acknowledgements | 6 |
| Introduction | 7 |
| The Renaissance of Waka Taua | 11 |
| Building a Waka Taua | 18 |
| Parts of the Waka | 42 |
| Paddling the Waka | 59 |
| Appendix: Paddling Instructions | 70 |
| Glossary | 72 |
| Recommended Reading | 76 |

# Acknowledgements

Firstly, I would like to acknowledge the co-operation of the Turangawaewae Marae Committee, which generously allowed me to use photos taken during the 1999 Turangawaewae Regatta within this book.

Special thanks also to Dr Roger Neich of the Auckland Museum for help and advice during the early stages of writing the book, and to Robin Reed for sharing his vast knowledge of the northern waka taua *Ngatokimatawhaorua*.

# Introduction

**W**aka Taua is an introduction to the construction and use of the Maori war canoe, the waka taua. It focuses on time-honoured building techniques and knowledge passed down from one generation to the next, and supplements this traditional information with descriptions and narratives from the diaries and letters of early visitors, settlers and ethnographers, along with paintings and sketches from both professional and amateur artists. There are variations to the general information offered within these pages — some tribes preferred original styles of carving and design, for example, and I don't profess to have covered every regional difference. Yet a review covering anything but the more obvious variations is perhaps best left for a more scholarly text.

My own introduction to waka taua was probably typical of many New Zealanders. The first waka taua I saw was during a family visit to Auckland Museum. The magnificent waka *Te Toki-a-Tapiri* seemed to dominate the Maori

**The war canoe *Taheretikitiki* at Devonport, Auckland, ca. 1890.** (AUCKLAND MUSEUM/TE PAPA WHAKAHIKU)

7

## Waka Taua

court, its impressive size exaggerated further in the eyes of a young boy. Then, in my late teens, I glimpsed a waka on the Waikato River just north of Hamilton — the crew was doubtless training for one of the annual Ngaruawahia Festival races. I saw the canoe for no more than ten seconds, but the sight of the paddle blades flashing in unison, the water churning behind every paddle and the foam path behind the waka has stayed with me ever since.

The next time I saw a waka taua was at the sesquicentennial celebration of the Treaty of Waitangi in the Bay of Islands, in 1990. Nineteen impressive waka were built for these celebrations. The sight of so many waka on the water together at Waitangi was awe-inspiring — even for those watching the event on television. (Anne Nelson's book *Waka Maori* has a number of wonderful photos from this event.)

My next encounter with waka taua occurred in early 1998 when I visited master canoe builder Matahi Brightwell in Gisborne. While I was there Matahi took me to Whangara to see the waka taua *Nukutaimemeha*, which was nearing completion under his expert guidance. At 45 m long, it is probably the largest waka taua ever built, with an imposing hull made by laminating lengths of timber from several totara trees.

The visit to see (and help paint, even if only for a couple of hours) *Nukutaimemeha* at Whangara was the spur I needed to start finding out more about waka taua.

Once I started my research, it soon became obvious that information on waka taua was dispersed throughout many books and journals, some of them long out of print, some of them just too full of technical detail for the general reader. The more I read, the more I realised that there was a need for an introductory book that gave more information about waka taua than could be found on a museum label or in a general book on Maori culture. So, after numerous false starts and rewrites, here is my offering. I hope you enjoy this book and learn something from it.

*Jeff Evans*

The author helping with work on the mighty waka taua *Nukutaimemeha*, at Whangara.

# The Renaissance of Waka Taua

The sight of a waka taua being paddled at full speed, the crew putting every last ounce of energy into propelling their craft through the water, is truly impressive. How many people watching such a scene have imagined what it must have been like to be part of a crew racing to attack an enemy pa, or felt a shiver up their spine as they imagined being a defender on land waiting for the onslaught? A waka taua in full flight is a sight to make your heart skip a beat — power, beauty and death all rolled into one.

The same feeling of awe is experienced when you see a waka taua up close, whether it be beached during Waitangi Day celebrations or at rest in a museum. Of course you have to show respect for the waka and refrain from touching it without permission, yet you can still see the strength, artistry and skill that the canoe builder possessed. The precision of the joinery, the ingenuity of design, the elegance of the hull's lines and the finish of the carving are all cause for admiration, and create a lasting impression.

Traditionally, as in the present day, waka taua were generally owned by the hapu, or sub-tribe, rather than by an individual. Their construction called on the efforts of many people either directly or

## Waka Taua

Tohunga tarai waka with a haumi section, an addition to the hull, nearing completion. The photograph was probably taken in the Taupo area during the 1930s.
(FATHER JAN BEEK; AUCKLAND MUSEUM/TE PAPA WHAKAHIKU)

indirectly, and really united a community. Expert canoe builders, known as tohunga tarai waka, would oversee the project and often complete the more important aspects of the construction themselves; expert carvers were often contracted in from other tribes to do the finishing work; tohunga, or priests, would be called upon to offer prayers at appropriate times in the construction; workmen would need to dedicate themselves to the project for months on end, often miles from the village and their loved ones; kiekie and other fibrous plants would need to be gathered and woven into sails and rope for lashing, often by the women and elderly; raupo would be collected as caulking material (and in some cases for sails), and kokowai and shark-liver oil as ingredients for the paint; villagers would also have to prepare and cook food for the workers in special ovens separate from the village cooking — and so on — all the while with the usual everyday needs of village life continuing.

# The Renaissance of Waka Taua

A large waka taua could take two years or more to complete, from the selection and cutting of the giant totara or kauri tree to be used for the hull, to the whakainu waka, or launching of the waka. All the while, the success of the project depended upon the tribe working together towards the common goal.

Once completed, the canoe was often available for community uses in addition to its main purpose of transporting warriors to and from battle. Only the most important and tapu canoes were reserved purely for war. Some of the less important waka taua were used for social visits, trading, or even fishing — once the carved tauihu and taurapa (prow- and stern-pieces) had been removed and stored.

Early European visitors and immigrants to New Zealand often recorded their impressions of waka taua in their journals and letters home. It is clear that the sight of a fleet of waka taua at sea must have been truly awe-inspiring. The following account by Major R.A. Cruise of the 84th Regiment Foot, from his *Journal of a ten months' residence in New Zealand*, describes such a fleet returning to the Bay of Islands in 1820 after a successful raid:

> *The fleet was composed of about fifty canoes, many of them seventy or eighty feet long, and a few less than sixty. Their prows, sides, and stern posts were handsomely ornamented with a profusion of feathers; and they generally carried two sails made of straw matting. They were filled with warriors, who stood up and shouted as they passed our boat, and held up several human heads as trophies of their success.*
>
> *The largest canoe we saw was eighty-four feet long, six feet wide, and five feet deep . . . It was made of a single kauri tree hollowed out, and raised about two feet with planks firmly tied together and to the main trunk, with pieces of the flax-plant*

## Waka Taua

*inserted through them. The crevices were filled with reeds to make the canoe watertight. A post fifteen feet high rose from the stern, which together with the sides was carved in openwork, painted red, and fringed with a profusion of black feathers. The chief sat at the stern, and steered the canoe, which was impelled by the united force of ninety naked men, who were painted and ornamented with feathers. Three others, standing upon the thwart-sticks, regulated the strokes of the paddles by repeating, with violent gestures, a song in which they were joined by every one in the vessel. The canoe moved with astonishing rapidity, causing the water to foam on either side of it; and we have observed other war-canoes cross the Bay of Islands in perfect safety when it was thought imprudent to lower the ship's boats.*

It is through such eyewitness descriptions, the drawings and paintings of early visitors, as well as the various artefacts held in museums and private collections (for example the sole remaining Maori canoe sail, which is currently held in the British Museum), that we are able to form a strong impression of the traditional waka taua. Without these priceless snippets of information, it is certain that irreplaceable knowledge would have been lost.

From the middle of the nineteenth century, however, the decline of the waka taua as a symbol of tribal mana in Maori society was frighteningly quick. As the European colonisation of New Zealand gathered pace from the 1840s onwards, more and more sailing ships began to ply the coastal waters, and these vessels were able to carry more cargo than the waka, and required fewer crew. The expansion of New Zealand's road and rail networks, and the relative ease of movement these afforded eventually led the waka taua to fall out of everyday use. By the end of the New Zealand Wars in the 1870s, the great fighting waka had had their day.

# The Renaissance of Waka Taua

*Flotte de Guerre à la Nouvelle-Zélande.* First published in 1839, this extraordinary engraving by Louis Auguste de Sainson (who accompanied the French navigator Dumont d'Urville on his voyages around New Zealand) shows a fleet of upwards of twenty waka taua, probably on the way to raid an enemy tribe. (ALEXANDER TURNBULL LIBRARY, NATIONAL LIBRARY OF NEW ZEALAND/TE PUNA MATAURANGA O AOTEAROA, WELLINGTON)

Te Puea Herangi, the great Waikato leader, was the first to initiate a revival in the fortunes of the giant waka. Princess Te Puea saw the revival of waka taua on the Waikato River as a way to strengthen her people's longstanding spiritual and worldly ties to the river. In 1936 she organised the salvage of the hull of the waka *Te Winika* from near the mouth of the Waikato River, and its reconstruction. The broken hull had lain on the banks of the Waikato since the early 1860s, when, during the New Zealand Wars, Gustavus von Tempsky and his Forest Rangers had destroyed it and a number of other waka to prevent warriors from moving up and down the river. At the same time as *Te Winika* was rebuilt, two more waka taua, *Aotea* and *Takitimu* (since renamed *Tumanako* and *Te Rangatahi* respectively) were built to accompany *Te Winika* for the 1940 Treaty of Waitangi centennial celebrations. (The impressive waka taua *Ngatokimatawhaorua* was also built for the centennial celebrations by the people of Tai Tokerau.)

## Waka Taua

**Governor-General Viscount Galway arriving on *Te Winika* for the opening of King Koroki's new whare, Turongo, at Turangawaewae Marae, Ngaruawahia, in 1938.**
(Auckland Museum/Te Papa Whakahiku)

Despite funding problems resulting from broken government promises, and the outbreak of World War II, Te Puea's project was a huge success — thanks in no small part to the combined efforts of her people — and all three waka were finished in time for the celebrations.

The same aim of kotahitanga (bringing people together through a common cause) was adopted for the Kaupapa Waka project which became such an integral part of the 1990 sesquicentennial celebration of the Treaty of Waitangi. In all, nineteen new waka were built for the celebrations by tribes from the North Island, the South Island and the Chatham Islands. Some tribes used traditional construction techniques, others used modern materials such as fibreglass and epoxy glues, while others struck a balance between old and new by using laminated hulls built up from the timber of several logs.

# The Renaissance of Waka Taua

As had been hoped, the process of building the waka, training as crew members, and the emotion of being with their waka on the water during the celebrations was an incredible experience for many of the participants, a large number of whom lived in the larger cities away from their tribal roots.

Some of the tribes also took the opportunity to make their war canoe noa, or free from tapu. This was done with the help of elders or priests who performed appropriate rituals and prayers. Once the whakanoa ceremony was completed, both women and non-Maori were invited to participate in the project, thus involving and strengthening the wider community as well.

The twentieth-century renaissance in building waka taua has been largely the result of the dedication of a few far-sighted individuals with a dream. Because of them, waka like those that once commonly cruised our waters in large numbers can still be seen. These waka, modern versions of the graceful waka that carried warriors to war in the nineteenth century and before, are a strong connection for many modern-day Maori to their past, and perhaps for some, to their future. During both the 1940 centennial celebrations of the signing of the Treaty of Waitangi and, especially, the 1990 sesquicentennial celebrations, the waka taua came to be a powerful symbol of Maori tribal identity and pride. Now, not only do waka taua symbolise the unity of a tribe, they also symbolise a proud, strong and defiant people. On the world stage, waka taua have represented New Zealand at such events as the America's Cup at Fremantle and the South Pacific Festival of the Arts in the Cook Islands. Waka taua help set Maori apart from the rest — not only in New Zealand but in the world at large.

# Building a Waka Taua

## The Work of the Master Canoe Builder

In the years before Europeans brought their steel tools to New Zealand, the construction of a waka taua was a major undertaking for a tohunga tarai waka, or canoe-building expert.

The first task was to select a sound tree suitable for the hull. This could take some time as the tohunga checked over a number of prospective trees, but usually he would have a range of suitable trees narrowed down in his mind before he began. Sometimes a suitable tree could not be found within the tribe's boundaries, and then a neighbouring iwi might be approached with an offer of trade for a desirable log. If agreement was reached, the villagers would then drag or float the log to the construction site. If an appropriate tree happened to be on tribal land at a considerable distance from the village, the villagers might plant crops near it to sustain the workforce during the weeks or months they would spend at the site.

When the day came to cut down the chosen tree, the senior tohunga, or priest, performed sacred rituals and prayers, asking

# Building a Waka Taua

the guardian of the forest, Tane Mahuta, for permission to take the tree. He also asked that the workmen be protected while they toiled in Tane's domain, Te Wao-nui-o-Tane. The tree was then felled and the crown and any branches removed, and preliminary work began on the hull to lighten it. The partially hollowed hull might then be dragged to the construction site for completion.

When the hull and other parts of the waka were complete, they were usually seasoned by immersion in either fresh or salt water, or sometimes in mud. After that the most skilled of the workmen would carefully piece the waka together, and the last stage would be to paint it. At last the waka taua would be ready to be launched, once again under the guidance of the tribal priests.

## Selecting an Appropriate Tree

Selecting a suitable tree was crucial to building a strong waka. Generally tribes south of Auckland favoured totara, while tribes from Auckland north preferred kauri. Both timbers had the advantage of being relatively free of knots, and could be cut easily using stone adzes. Tohunga tarai waka sometimes used other trees, such as kahikatea and rimu, but only if they could not find suitable totara or kauri.

Tohunga examined prospective trees carefully for signs of imperfection. These included wide flangy roots, which indicated heart shakes (major cracks within the tree) and twisted grain; spongy bark, which indicated that there would be too much sapwood and that the grain would be weak; and decaying roots, which suggested major

A stand of kauri at Ruakaka, in Northland. The first limb of the tallest tree branches out an impressive 26 m from the ground.
(REED PUBLISHING PHOTOGRAPHIC LIBRARY)

## Waka Taua

problems further up the tree. Positive signs included trees growing close to the valley floor, which were usually better nourished and had a strong grain, and trees with thick bark, which were mature and had a close, strong grain.

Once a tree was selected by the tohunga, the ground around it was often cleared of scrub and small bushes to show that it was taunahatia, or had been chosen by one of the tribe for a future project. If the tree was to be left standing for a period of time after its selection, a length of bark was sometimes stripped from one side of its trunk. The tree would then start to decay along the strip, which reduced the amount of effort required to adze out the hull. Young trees were sometimes randomly treated in this way as well, so that by the time they reached maturity a large portion of the trunk would be hollow.

### Felling the Tree

It is not hard to imagine the immense effort required to cut down a large totara or kauri with stone adzes. Early European reports suggested that it may have taken anything from two to five days of back-breaking work. One technique was for a pair of men to chip away at the tree trunk to form two parallel horizontal channels, up to as much as a metre apart, right around the trunk. Once these channels had been completed, the workmen employed a heavy adze to remove the timber between them. This process was repeated at deeper and deeper levels until the tree had been cut through. Sometimes controlled fire was also used at this stage to assist in this work.

When the tree was lying on the forest floor, the priests would return and demonstrate their thanks to Tane Mahuta by placing offerings, often ferns or cooked food, on the stump. They then stepped aside to let the workmen begin to hollow out the trunk.

# Building a Waka Taua

The stone adzes used in canoe building were called toki tarai waka, and they came in different sizes and forms. Naturally the biggest and heaviest adzes were used for cutting down the tree and roughing out the hull. Next, lighter adzes were employed to finish hollowing out the hull and to shape the outside, as well as much of the initial work required to prepare the rauawa, or topstrakes, the tauihu and taurapa. As the work got more delicate, so did the size and weight of the adzes employed. The finishing adzes were sometimes of pounamu (greenstone), a highly treasured stone.

A canoe builder displaying traditional and modern adzes. (AUCKLAND MUSEUM/TE PAPA WHAKAHIKU)

## Hollowing Out the Tree

Once the tree had been felled, the tohunga checked that it was indeed sound, and that the trunk had not been badly damaged in the fall. After it had been passed, the first job was to remove the crown and branches from the trunk, often using a combination of fire and adzing.

First, a controlled fire, using sticks of a timber such as tawa, rewarewa or taraire, was lit at the point where a cut was to be made. When the fire had burnt 3–5 cm into the wood, the burning sticks were removed and the burnt area was dowsed with water. This was to cool it, so that the adzes, used next, wouldn't be exposed to excessive heat, which might cause them to crack or shatter. Once the burnt area was judged cool enough, the workmen chipped away at it until it had been removed, then the procedure

## Waka Taua

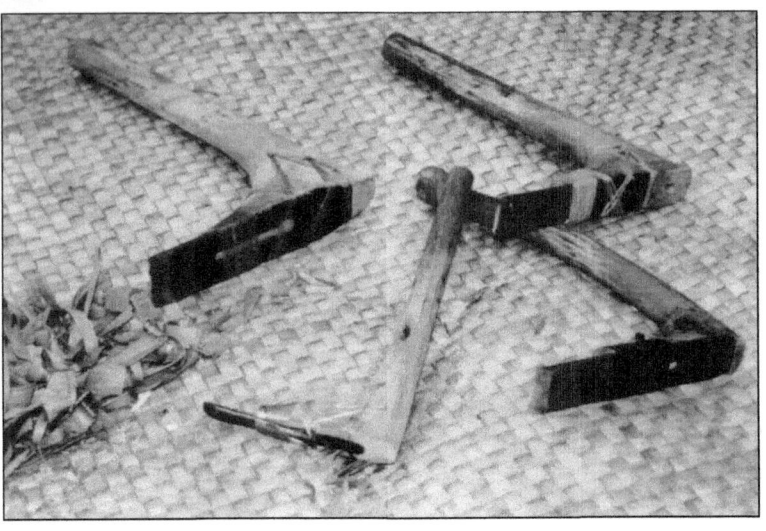

Contemporary canoe builders fashion adzes using modern materials such as plane blades and nylon fishing line. It is interesting to compare the bevels of these contemporary adzes, which face up, with that of the traditional adze, shown on page 21 (on left of picture), which faces down.

was repeated. It is said that this process was faster than working solely with adzes and also safer than letting the fire do all the work.

After the workers had removed the head and the branches, the tree was ready for its preliminary shaping. It was usual for the waka to be shaped with the butt end of the tree forming the bow, because the bow of a waka taua was appreciably wider than the stern, and the tree tapered from the butt up. The amount of adzing that was done at this stage depended largely on the distance and quality of the terrain between the site of the tree and the village. A relatively smooth and short trip meant that the tohunga could allow a fair portion of the hollowing and shaping to be completed in the forest. If, however, the tree was a long way from the village, or the terrain was challenging, then it was usually thought prudent to keep the trunk as solid as possible to try and avoid damage during haulage. The tohunga also had to make allowance in his calculations for the amount of timber that would be worn away through friction during the haul.

Once the tohunga had decided on a practical thickness for the hull, the inside was roughed out with adzes, leaving a bruised and splintered surface. This rough surface was then further reduced by fire, and the process was repeated until the optimum 'dragging' thickness was reached. Sometimes a number of bulkheads were left in the hull at this stage to provide additional strength during the hauling. The last consideration for the tohunga was the positioning

# Building a Waka Taua

of two posts that were sometimes left standing inside the hull. These were known as putiki or maunga taura, and they were used for securing the hauling ropes.

When the inside of the hull was completed to this stage it was carefully turned over and the outside was adzed with the large, heavy adzes, until the waka's approximate shape was attained. After this, the hull was usually seasoned for a number of months so that the timber would strengthen and the form consolidate; this might be done in a moist trench, or the hull might be dragged to a river or the seashore for the purpose.

## Other Work in the Forest

At the same time as the hull was being prepared, numerous other projects were also progressing. Specialist workmen split and adzed long boards out of single logs to form the rauawa and taka (battens). Often elaborately carved, rauawa were lengths of timber (sometimes more than 20 or 25 m long, depending on the overall length of the waka taua) that were formed to raise the height of the waka's sides. They were lashed edge to edge along the top of the hull's sides from the front to the back. While there are recorded instances of two or more rauawa being stacked on each side of a waka, it was usual to have only one rauawa per side. Taka of equal length to the rauawa were

A tohunga tarai waka at work.
(ALEXANDER TURNBULL LIBRARY, NATIONAL LIBRARY OF NEW ZEALAND/TE PUNA MATAURANGA O AOTEAROA, WELLINGTON)

 ## Waka Taua

**A haumi kokomo being fitted to the hull of a waka taua. Traditionally, all the measurements and cuts were judged by eye.**
(AUCKLAND MUSEUM/TE PAPA WHAKAHIKU)

then placed along both the inside and the outside of the join between the hull and the rauawa so as to make it watertight. The inner pair of battens were sometimes known as paiwai.

Other workmen might be ordered to shape a haumi kokomo, or false end, for the waka. These were necessary if the hull proved to be shorter than the required length, or if one end of the trunk had been damaged during felling or hauling. Work on the tauihu and taurapa was also started early in the piece, to ensure they, too, were completed by the time the waka was ready to be launched.

# Building a Waka Taua

## HAULING THE TREE FROM THE FOREST

Although all the able-bodied members of a village might be called in to clear a path and help haul a tree to the work site, things could still go wrong. A rope might snap under strain, or the tree might twist and roll out of control on an incline and smash against boulders. To reduce the possibility of such a calamity, an experienced tohunga would take care to select the safest route, which was not necessarily the shortest.

Between two and four sizeable ropes would be used to haul the semi-finished hull from the forest. These ropes were made from the dried leaves of the ti torere (*Cordyline banksii*) or ti kauka (*Cordyline australis*), usually plaited in the five-strand method known as raura. The ropes, as thick as an adult's wrist and very durable, were attached to the putiki at both the bow and stern ends. Complementary to the ropes were smooth cylindrical skids (neke, ngaro or rango), which were placed under the hull. The favourite

Canoe builders using a team of bullocks to drag a haumi section along a path cleared through dense forest, probably in the 1930s. As was traditionally the case, neke, or skids, are being used to reduce the effort required.
(AUCKLAND MUSEUM/TE PAPA WHAKAHIKU)

# Waka Taua

timber for the skids was either puahou, also known as houhou (*Pseudopanax arboreum*), which was renowned for being smooth and slippery, or ti kauka.

Before the haul began, the work crew would be split into three main groups: the first comprised the men assigned to hauling on the ropes; the second was responsible for ensuring the canoe stayed upright; and the third, smaller group had the task of picking up the skids after the hull had passed over them and carrying them to the front.

During the haul, which might cover anything up to eight kilometres in a single day, depending on the terrain, the workers were encouraged by a kaea. The kaea's responsibility was to chant rangi waka, or waka-hauling songs, which were chosen for their appropriateness to the terrain being traversed. For instance, songs and chants with long syllables were chosen for tough uphill work when brute force was needed, and chants with shorter syllables would be sung on the flat or downhill sections. Experienced kaea were also known to change the words of the odd verse to bring in topical subjects and enliven the day's toil.

## Finishing Work

Finally, after much effort and perhaps many days' hard toil, the waka reached its final adzing site, where construction would be completed. Here, the senior tohunga tarai waka took charge. If the wood had not yet been seasoned, the tohunga supervised as the hull was lowered into a trench, or perhaps deposited in a river or the sea, where it would be left for several months.

While the waka was being seasoned, a temporary shelter was constructed to protect the hull from the elements once the final work commenced. This structure also served to mark the site as a tapu

# Building a Waka Taua

Canoe sections being seasoned in a river near Ngaruawahia. While salt water is considered superior by some for seasoning timber, many tribes lived too far from the sea for this to be practicable.
(AUCKLAND MUSEUM/TE PAPA WHAKAHIKU)

area, where those without business should not venture. Once the tohunga tarai waka judged the hull to be ready for further work, the next task was the final adzing. This was carried out by experienced men whose skill ensured that the inside of the canoe would be perfectly symmetrical. They worked without the assistance of either drawn plans or measuring tapes.

Generally the inside of the waka was adzed smooth and finished with sandstone or sharkskin 'sandpaper'. In some parts of the country a hole was bored in the bottom of the hull, slightly forward of the waka's mid-point. This was so that any water that splashed in could be let out once the craft had been beached. The hole would be tightly closed with a wooden plug.

The tohunga had a choice of several finishes for the outside of the hull, including a scalloped pattern, and another said to resemble fish scales. Others favoured a smooth outer surface to match the

# Waka Taua

**The outside of a waka taua's hull was often given a scalloped finish, which was believed to reduce the hold of the water. The style shown here is called ngatoa.**

inside of the hull. The reasoning behind the scalloped finish is explained in the following excerpt from a letter written by Hare Hongi, a former student at the northern whare wananga at Waitaha and Native Land Court interpreter, in 1911:

*Greeting! When a boy I took a particular interest in canoe-building operations, tarai waka (canoe-hewing). I was struck by the fact that the Maori deliberately left the outside of his canoe widely grooved with narrow intervening ridges.*

*I therefore asked one of our old tohunga tarai waka (canoe-hewing experts) what the object was in doing so. He explained to me that the toki umarua (double-shouldered adze) was specially made to pare-ngarungaru the exterior of the canoe (to prevent the water from clinging to the canoe, and so impeding its progress). The object, therefore, was to break up the water*

# Building a Waka Taua

which the canoe was passing through, and so to give it greater speed, or to make the business of paddling easier.

There may be science in this. Note the polished exterior of the pakeha racing-skiffs. Does not the water cling to the sides and act as a break from end to end?

Kia ora. HARE HONGI.

P.S. The interior of the canoe was comparatively smooth.

Once the outside of the hull was finished, the next step for the tohunga was to oversee the fixing of the haumi kokomo (if it was required) to the hull proper. Many waka taua were lengthened with a haumi kokomo, and a significant number of them were fitted with one at each end. The join between the hull and the haumi kokomo was similar to a mortice and tenon joint, with the tongue section usually part of the main hull, and the slot in the haumi kokomo.

A three-ply rope of either ti kauka or kiekie was usually used to secure the haumi kokomo to the hull. The rope was passed through adjacent holes in the hull and haumi, which were either drilled or hewn with a chisel. Channels were often cut into the timber on the outside of the hull to allow the ropes to be countersunk. The primary reason for using this technique was to avoid any unnecessary wear and tear on the fibre when the waka was

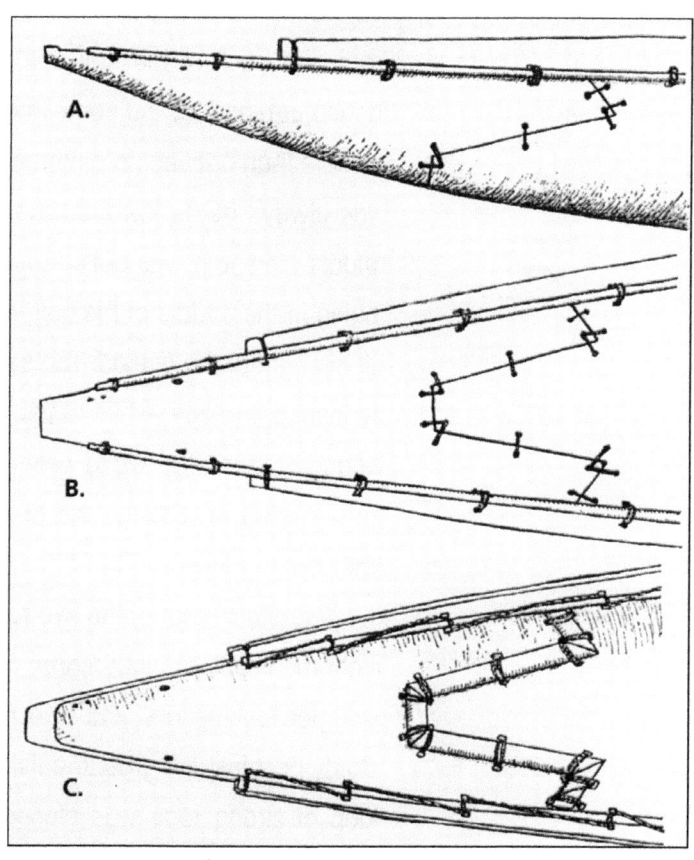

The haumi kokomo join of a canoe hull, drawn by Miss E. Richardson (from Elsdon Best, *The Maori Canoe*).

A. A side view of the hull.

B. The view from below.

C. The view from above.

(MUSEUM OF NEW ZEALAND/TE PAPA TONGAREWA)

## Waka Taua

being dragged ashore or being buffeted by strong seas. It also helped limit the drag on the waka when it was in motion.

To increase watertightness, strips of raupo leaf were usually placed between the two joining edges, and hune (pappus of the seeds of the raupo) was driven tightly into any remaining cracks with a hardwood wedge. Finally, a batten was placed over the join on the inside of the hull.

Once the haumi kokomo was firmly secured to the main hull, the next step was to lash the rauawa, or topstrakes, in position. First, strips of raupo were laid along the niao, or top edge of the hull, and held in place with temporary flax ties threaded through the kowhao, or lashing holes. Next a rauawa was placed along the top edge of the hull. At this stage, because the rauawa was hewn flat rather than curved like the hull, only a short length in the middle was in contact with the hull — the ends protruding from the front and back of the hull somewhat — and it was temporarily lashed in place. (If, as sometimes occurred, the rauawa consisted of more than one length of timber, the join between the two lengths was always made towards one end of the hull rather than in the middle. This join was butted and tightly lashed. If the rauawa was joined in the middle of the hull, it would severely weaken the overall strength of the waka.) The second rauawa was then temporarily lashed in place, while at the same time a length of timber was wedged across the waka between the two rauawa to stop them from folding in. Finally, the two rauawa were ready to be firmly lashed into place.

The attachment of the two rauawa was generally performed by eight men split into four teams of two — each team being responsible for lashing one end of a rauawa. The first job was to set a sturdy post into the ground outside the end of each rauawa. Then a loop of strong rope was placed around the pole, passed across

# Building a Waka Taua

the hull, and looped round the opposite rauawa. A stick was then placed between the two sides of the rope, forming a tourniquet, and repeatedly turned until the rauawa started to pull across. The lashing was completed from the middle section outwards, finishing at the ends of the rauawa. As the work progressed, additional lengths of timber were wedged crossways between the two rauawa to stop them folding in. Once the ends of the rauawa had been pulled into position, a taumanu, or thwart, was lashed in position as additional support to keep the rauawa in place and tight.

The temporary lashings, now all firmly in position, were further tightened by the tohunga with the introduction of small wooden wedges, called matiti, which were driven into the lashing holes. This was to ensure that the lashings did not slacken and allow the rauawa to pull away from the hull.

With the rauawa in place and the temporary lashings complete, the tohunga could commence the final part of the topstrake fitting, introducing the inner and outer battens.

The men paired off again, but this time their work progressed from the ends of the rauawa back towards the middle of the hull, rather than from the centre out. The first step was for one of the workmen to knock out the outermost matiti and thread the kaha, or lashing cord, through the lower hole to his partner. The kaha was then passed back through the upper hole and pulled as tight as

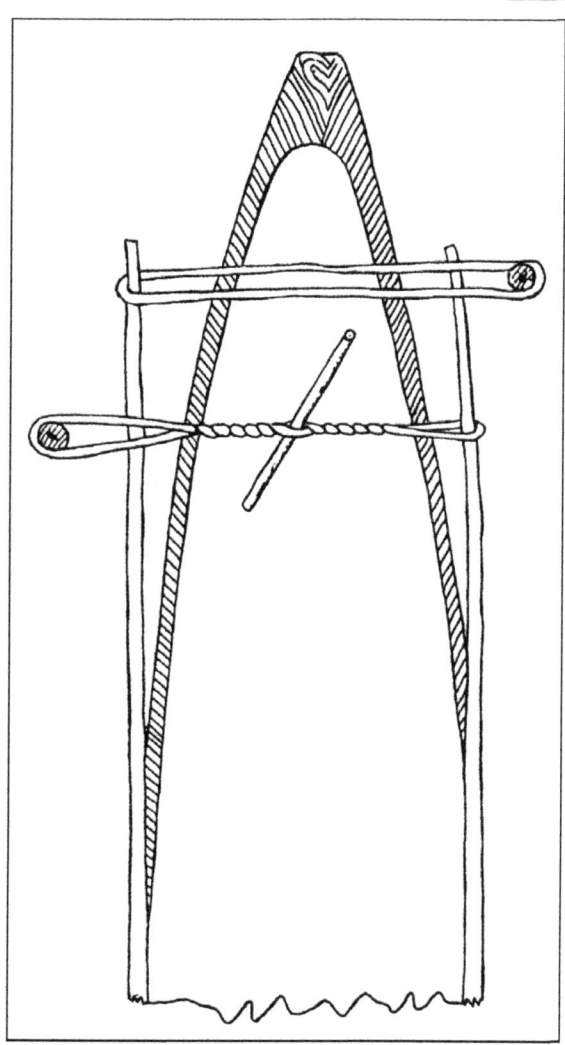

A drawing by Miss E. Richardson showing the method of clamping home the topstrakes, or rauawa, of a canoe (from Elsdon Best, *The Maori Canoe*). (MUSEUM OF NEW ZEALAND/TE PAPA TONGAREWA)

## Waka Taua

possible. To achieve this, the Maori used a Y-shaped tool called a tanekaha or mimiro, which was designed to lever maximum tension on the rope. Use of the tanekaha is mentioned by Elsdon Best in his book *The Maori Canoe*:

> The end of the cord being secured, the man in the canoe passes the end through to the outside, where it is seized by his mate and passed back through the other hole, so that it encloses and grips the batten; this process being repeated until two or three turns of the cord have been passed through the holes, which are thereby pretty well blocked. But each time the cord is so passed through a hole it is tightened by the use of an implement termed a mimiro among the Ngati-Porou folk, and a tanekaha by Tuhoe.
>
> This item is a forked stick shaped like the letter Y, and is a piece of tough or hard wood, such as toatoa and manuka. The two arms of the Y are the handles by which it is manipulated. When the cord is pulled through the hole by one man, he winds

**Using the tanekaha, or mimiro, to tighten the lashings. Drawing by A.H. Messenger (from Elsdon Best, *The Maori Canoe*).**
(MUSEUM OF NEW ZEALAND/ TE PAPA TONGAREWA)

# Building a Waka Taua

*it round the shank of the mimiro, runs the free part of the cord up to the end of the handles, round which he makes a few turns with it, and then hands the apparatus to his companion. The latter grasps the handles, holding the twisted cord under the one hand, places the shank of the implement against the gunwale of the canoe — i.e., the top of the top-strake, which is now the gunwale — and which serves as a fulcrum, and presses down on the handles. By this means he can put a very heavy strain upon the cord, which is stretched and tightened until absolutely rigid and immovable. This strain is held by the man with the mimiro, while the other, armed with a mallet, drives a wooden toggle into the hole in order to plug it and prevent the cord slackening. The cord is then unwound from the implement, passed through the other hole, and again tightened by the same process, whereupon the toggle is knocked out and driven into the other hole; or a second toggle is driven into the latter hole, then the first one is knocked out. The lashing of one set of holes being completed, the final passage of the cord being from the outside to the inside of the canoe, the cord is carried along against the inside of the canoe some 9 in. to 12 in. [23 to 30 cm] to the next set of holes, which are lashed in the same manner.*

Once this process was complete and the rauawa firmly in place, the tohunga caulked any gaps left in the lashing holes with a tacky gum called pia houhou or ware houhou. This gum was extracted from the houhou tree and smeared onto either flax fibre or the inner bark of hoheria (*Hoheria populnea*), which was then wedged into place.

The next task was to lash the remaining taumanu in position. These taumanu were solid lengths of timber, often fashioned from

## Waka Taua

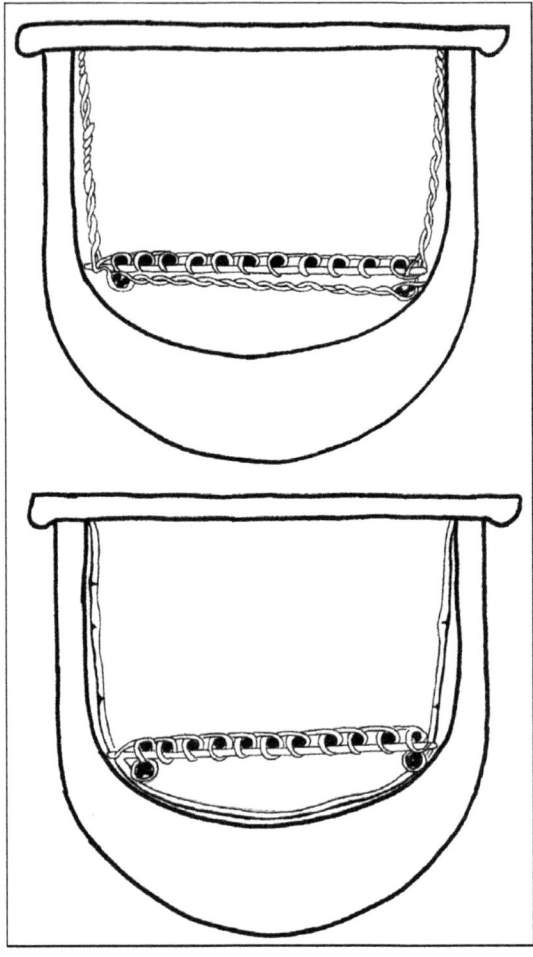

**Common methods of supporting the rahoraho, or flooring, of a waka taua: above, using ake vines to support the cross rods; and below, using straight rods lashed to the cross rods.**

totara or matai, which spanned the width of the waka every few feet along its entire length. Once lashed tightly to the upper edges of the rauawa, the taumanu served to keep the hull rigid. They were also used as bracing by the paddlers, who would use their knees and their lower backs to wedge themselves between the taumanu in front of and behind them.

Occasionally taumanu featured detailed carvings on their surface. It is possible that these carved taumanu were reserved for important men of chiefly rank, or perhaps for priests, and that the carvings were to warn others of the tapu associated with that particular position.

The waka's steersman was assigned to the rearmost taumanu, from where he could guide the waka using the long steering paddle. The thwart directly in front of the steersman was reserved for the principal man on the waka. Larger waka were able to comfortably hold four or more men between thwarts, with the outer two men paddling and the others ready to relieve them when fatigue set in.

Once all the taumanu were lashed into place, and the tauihu and taurapa firmly secured to the hull and square-cut ends of the rauawa, the rahoraho or flooring was put in position. The rahoraho, consisting of thin rods of manuka lying fore and aft along the length of the waka, was held in place by one of two methods.

In the first method two long rods, one on either side of the hull, were supported by ake vines that had been lashed tightly under the taumanu. Poles were then tied across the hull horizontally at regular intervals, and the manuka flooring secured to these. In the

# Building a Waka Taua

second method two straight rods, one on either side of the hull, were lashed under the taumanu and used to support the cross pieces on which the flooring rested. In both cases the floor was secured just below the level of the lower edge of the rauawa. Openings spaced along the flooring, known as puna-wai or taingawai, served as bailing stations. Larger waka taua would typically have two such openings, while shorter waka might only have one.

A final touch given to some waka was the carving of a highly stylised figure on the underside of the hull, just below the position of the tauihu. This figure was called toiere or koneke, and it is sometimes said to be a guardian for both the waka and the crew.

## Painting the Waka

The hulls of waka taua were universally painted red (other than the puhoro design that was sometimes painted onto either end of the underside of the hull, although usually only under the tauihu). The paint was a mixture of shark-liver oil and either kokowai (red ochre) or burnt karamea clay. If karamea was used, the tohunga would first coat the surface to be painted with the juice of poporo leaves, which helped prevent the paint running.

Most of the pieces that had to be lashed in to place, such as the tauihu and taurapa, were painted beforehand. Kokowai or karamea paint was also used for the tauihu and taurapa if they were to be finished in red, and was usually applied using a brush of feathers (often hawk feathers). If, on the other hand, the tauihu and taurapa were to be painted black, as was often the case among northern tribes, the tohunga would apply a mixture of powdered charcoal, shark-liver oil and the sap from the leaf of the poporo tree. Another method was to submerge the carved pieces for two or three days in a bath of boiled and pounded hinau bark. In both cases the parts of the waka were commonly submerged for a

## Waka Taua

**The puhoro design painted under the prow (and sometimes under the stern) of waka taua is said to have been inspired by the reflection of the rippling water under the hull.**

couple of days in swamp waters rich in parapara, or sediment. If the hinau-bark method was used, the tohunga usually smothered the carving in oil or grease after it had been removed from the swamp to help seal the colour.

It seems that rauawa were universally painted red, while the taka, which covered the joining seam between the rauawa and the hull, were finished in black. White albatross feathers were spaced along the length of the taka, their quills being secured under the taka lashings.

Finally, the scrolled puhoro design on the hull just below the position of the tauihu and the taurapa might be painted (although, as mentioned above, the puhoro design seems to have been mostly applied to the front underside of the hull). The puhoro was generally finished in a combination of red, black and white paint — the

# Building a Waka Taua

white paint being a mixture of pulverised, burnt taioma, or pipeclay, mixed with shark-liver oil. It has been suggested that the puhoro design had its origins in the reflection of the rippling waters seen under the front of a waka on calm days.

## LAUNCHING THE WAKA TAUA

Launching a waka taua was a major event, following as it often did several months or even years of hard work. The ceremony was officiated over by the tribal priests, who had to perform a number of acts to prepare the waka for use.

Because the waka was built under strict tapu, the first task was to perform the kawa over it to prepare it for everyday use by the tribe. During this rite a branch, sometimes from the karangu shrub, was dipped in water and struck against the tauihu while the tohunga recited his incantations. If the recital of the prayer was word perfect, this was seen as a good omen. If, on the other hand, the priest made an error, then the waka would be considered an unlucky vessel, to be avoided if at all possible. The kawa was often followed by a priestess climbing into the waka, the final step in removing the tapu.

It was then time to launch the waka. As it was eased into the water the tohunga chanted a prayer to Tangaroa, guardian of the ocean, asking him to protect the waka and its crew while they were in his domain. When the waka was finally afloat, the crew embarked, strictly from the stern in accordance with age-old custom, and the waka's maiden voyage was under way.

After this voyage the waka was beached, stern first, and returned to the care of the tohunga tarai waka by the crew. The custom of beaching the waka stern first has been partly explained by Tuta Nihoniho, one of Elsdon Best's informants:

## Waka Taua

*In former times canoes of importance were brought to land stern first, being turned round just before reaching the beach, and backed in: the prow must not strike the beach. This relates to sea-going canoes only. Should the water be too rough near the beach to make the necessary turn, then it is effected out at sea, outside the breakers. It would be most unlucky to run the canoe ashore bow first.*

Beaching the canoe stern first also permitted a speedy departure.

The tohunga tarai waka, who would have taken special note of how the waka floated and the wake it left, now had an opportunity to make any final adjustments to the waka's shape before it was finally handed over to the tribe.

## Waka Unua: Double Canoes

Very little has been recorded about double canoes and their use by the Maori. Abel Tasman, who came across Aotearoa in 1642 and is recognised as the first European to visit this country, reported encountering a dozen or more double canoes while sheltering at Murderer's Bay (now Golden Bay) at the top of the South Island. Unfortunately few details were recorded about these waka, other than that they were double hulled and had a platform between the narrow hulls.

Sir Joseph Banks, the great botanist travelling on HMS *Endeavour* 127 years later, was the next European to leave a record of double canoes:

*November 1st, 1769: Just after nightfall we were under a small island [Whale Island, Bay of Plenty], from whence came off a*

# Building a Waka Taua

*Vaertuig en Gedaente der inwoonders van Selandia Nova.*

*large double canoe, or rather two canoes lashed together at a distance of about a foot, and covered with boards so as to make a kind of deck.*

James Cook noted that this was the first double canoe seen in New Zealand during the voyage.

Journal entries written during the early days of European–Maori interaction after Cook's visit suggest that by the time Europeans started to settle in New Zealand, permanent double canoes in the North Island were a thing of the past. Temporary double canoes, termed waka taurua, were still lashed together when needed, for instance when setting huge seine nets and the like, but the permanently lashed double canoe was for all intents and purposes confined to South Island waters.

One theory to explain the longer survival of permanent double canoes (called waka unua, hunua or huhunu) in the south revolves

An engraving, copied from a drawing by Isaac Gilsemanns, showing a double canoe seen during Tasman's visit to Aotearoa in 1642. Compared with later waka this one has very little ornamental carving on it, and while there is a short taurapa, or stern-piece, on each hull, there is no sign of a fitted tauihu (prow). The canoe does, however, have an external taka, or batten, covering the join between the nearside hull and topstrake. The paddles are interesting in that they clearly show the shape of the blades being used at that time.
(ALEXANDER TURNBULL LIBRARY, NATIONAL LIBRARY OF NEW ZEALAND/TE PUNA MATAURANGA O AOTEAROA, WELLINGTON)

## Waka Taua

around the lack of suitable trees in the populated areas of the South Island for building stable, single-hulled waka. The large totara and kauri trees readily found in the North Island were wide enough to provide a stable hull, while the circumference of the smaller southern trees made it imperative for waka to have a companion hull to contend with the rough waters found off the southern shores. Indeed, in Atholl Anderson's wonderful ethnohistory of southern Maori, *The Welcome of Strangers*, it is stated that Ngati Mamoe, who began to settle the top of the South Island about the turn of the sixteenth century, preferred waka unua over the faster single-hulled war canoes.

The following letter, written by F.V. Knapp of Nelson after speaking to an early settler (William Cole, who arrived from England on the *Lord Auckland* in 1842), gives what is almost certainly the last eyewitness account of double canoes anywhere in New Zealand.

> *In the late forties he [Cole] saw the Maori coming into port in their double canoes. According to his description, made to the writer some years ago, these were held together by poles lashed transversely and sufficiently wide apart to allow paddles being used between them, and conjointly bearing a central platform on which was stowed the produce for sale in the settlement. The canoes came up to the jetty at Auckland Point, probably coming from Motueka or Croixelles Harbour, either place being about 20 miles [32 kilometres] down Tasman Bay. Motueka at the time had a native population of about seven or eight hundred. Beyond weak eyesight and a slight deafness, Mr Cole still has the full use of his faculties. He is probably the only man living who has seen the Maori double canoe.*

# Building a Waka Taua

## Wharau: Canoe Sheds

When they were not in use, important waka taua were usually housed in open-sided canoe sheds known as wharau, or tawharau. Little physical evidence of these wharau has survived, but it is believed that they were gable roofed, and were obviously at least as long as the waka taua they sheltered. Early eyewitnesses, such as Joel Polack, stated that sometimes families, who were presumably responsible in some way for the waka's upkeep, resided on a mezzanine-type floor under the roof of the wharau.

While in the shed, the waka would be placed on rollers to prevent the hull from rotting underneath, and the taurapa and tauihu were removed and carefully stowed away. In particularly bad weather, a wall of manuka brush or a similar material was often lashed to the frame of the wharau to form a temporary wall that could protect the precious waka within.

The Ngati Paoa waka taua *Te Kotuiti Tuarua* in its wharau at Kaiaua Marae. The waka rests on its trailer, sheltered from the worst of the elements. The tauihu and taurapa are stored separately indoors.

# Parts of the Waka

## Tauihu: The Prow

The tauihu, or prow of a waka taua, was a beautifully designed and carved example of Maori art. Two main styles of tauihu were used for waka taua, along with a less common intermediate design.

The most common design was the pitau style, easily recognised by the full-bodied carved figure to the front, its tongue out in defiance and its arms stretched back (see illustration opposite). The other popular design was the tuere, which featured a thin central trapezoid-shaped panel with curving ribs extending diagonally through its length (see illustration page 44). Although the tuere is often referred to as the 'northern' style of tauihu, it was in fact used not only in the northern districts of Waikato, Auckland and Northland but also in the Bay of Plenty, the East Coast and Coromandel. The third style of tauihu, which was only occasionally encountered, included features from both the pitau and the tuere within its framework.

Within each of these three designs the general pattern was standard, only the size of the tauihu and the finishing surface work

# Parts of the Waka

providing any real licence for the carvers. As with the taurapa, tauihu were sometimes decorated for special occasions with pigeon or kaka feathers.

## Pitau

The pitau style of tauihu was perhaps the most commonly seen of the three designs. It consisted principally of a full-bodied figure leaning forward with its arms stretched backwards, leading the waka; a central panel stretching front to back, dominated by two large pitau, or spirals; and a splashguard featuring a carved figure looking back into the canoe, named Huaki. The pitau was often carved from a solid log, although some pitau in museum and private collections have lashings holding the arms in place.

The prow rested on the hull, and was butted against the ends of the rauawa. The battens that covered the joins between the two rauawa and the hull also covered the join between the tauihu and the hull. Tauihu originating in the central and southern parts of the North Island were usually painted the same red colour as the hull, while those from the more northern tribes were generally painted black.

This superb example of the pitau style of tauihu is held in the Auckland Museum collection. The carving is attributed to Te Ati Awa chief Wiremu Kingi Te Rangitake. (AUCKLAND MUSEUM/TE PAPA WHAKAHIKU; AM 7375)

# Waka Taua

**The waka taua *Taheretikitiki II* is adorned with a spectacular tauihu in the tuere style. In this photograph taken during the 1999 Ngaruawahia Regatta, the carved head, or parata, is surging through the water at the front of the waka.**

The name of this style of tauihu derived from the prominent double spirals carved within the central panel, which were themselves called pitau. Waka taua featuring this carving were sometimes called waka pitau. According to one source, the pitau were named after the young fronds of the manuka tree, and the studs between the spirals were said to represent the pinnae, or leaflets. The stylised figure that was usually seen between the two spirals was generally referred to as a manaia, although Ngati Porou called it tauroa.

## Tuere

The tuere's distinctive shape was easily distinguishable from the pitau style described above. While at first glance perhaps less spectacular than the pitau version, it provides a wonderful example of Maori carving and artistic balance.

The tuere was generally hewn out of four separate blocks — the base; the central panel; the rear splashguard with a carved human figure; and a realistically carved human head, known as a parata, that was lashed to the front underside of the hull just above the water line. The central panel was dominated by a long manaia

# Parts of the Waka

figure that formed an irregular broad rib curving up from the bottom edge of the panel, and culminating in a manaia head at the top front corner. Arms and legs extended from the body, reaching out to the outer edges of the panel. Both the central panel and the splashguard were fixed in place along grooves in the base plate, with dowels often inserted for added strength.

## INTERMEDIATE STYLE

Although it had features in common with both the tauihu already described, the intermediate style was sufficiently different to have its own classification. Similar to the pitau in basic design, with a bow-cover base, a central panel and a low splashguard across the rear edge, this style had a slightly elevated leading corner and lacked the realistically carved full-bodied figure out front. Instead, like the tuere, it featured a stylised manaia. Its other characteristics leaned more towards the pitau design, with the carving of the central panel comprising a double spiral separated by a manaia, and an upright figure positioned behind the rear splashboard. Like the pitau, it was usually formed from a solid log. Examples of the intermediate style of tauihu have been found in both the North Taranaki and Waipu areas.

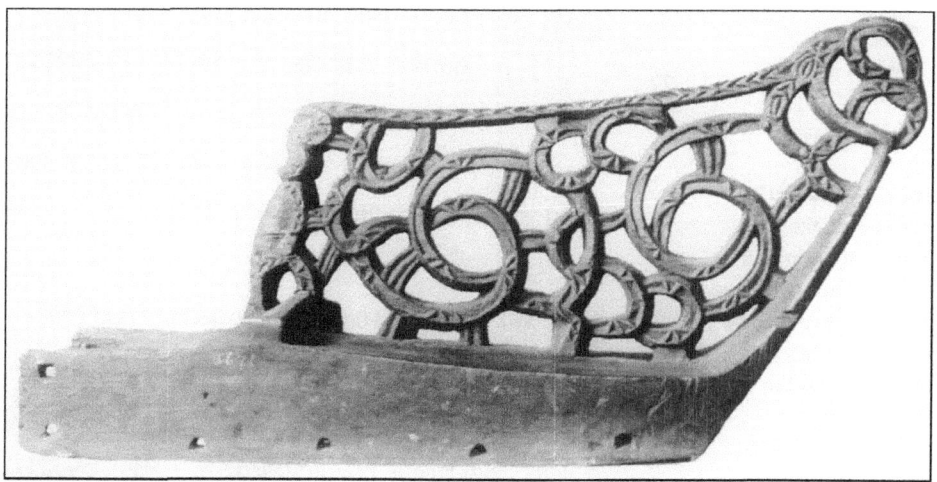

A fine tauihu in the intermediate style, originating from Mokau, Taranaki. (AUCKLAND MUSEUM/TE PAPA WHAKAHIKU; AM 5676)

# Waka Taua

**Formerly used to decorate waka taua participating in raids, ihiihi are now displayed at times of ceremony. Here, ihiihi reach forward from the waka taua *Tumanako*.**

## Ihiihi

During important ceremonial occasions, or when venturing out on raids, waka taua were often decorated with a pair of ihiihi (or hihi) made from slim rods of manuka or tanekaha. Each rod had a circular hoop tied to its forward extremity which was known as a karu atua, or eye of god. It is possible that in earlier times a diamond shape was formed within each hoop to represent the eyes. The significance of these karu atua has been forgotten, but they originally may have been used in navigation. Bunches of albatross or gannet feathers at intervals of approximately 30 cm along the rod's length completed its decoration.

George Forster, who visited Queen Charlotte Sound in 1773, mentions seeing:

*the war canoe in which a war expedition had been made; it had a carved head ornamented with bunches of brown feathers, and a double pronged fork projected from it, on which the heart of their slain enemy was transfixed.*

Parts of the Waka

## TAURAPA: THE STERN-PIECE

The taurapa, or rapa as it was sometimes called, was the stern-piece of a waka taua. Elaborately carved, the taurapa (along with the tauihu) was undoubtedly the pinnacle of the carver's art prior to the introduction of metal tools to New Zealand. Often carved from totara or matai, taurapa were prized possessions that were carefully stored when not in use, and whenever possible passed from one generation to the next.

When looking at a taurapa, the initial impression is of a highly carved panel well reinforced by a pair of strong curved ribs. These ribs continue the graceful lines of the hull, extending from the base of the taurapa to a point approximately three-quarters of the way up the panel. The ribs, which usually feature light surface carving, gradually taper as they sweep up the stern-piece until they meet the leading edge, where one or both of the ribs is often grasped by a manaia figure. A number of pitau can be seen on either side of the ribs, giving a balance to the carving.

There are at least two recorded accounts that explain the meaning of the rib design. The first claims that the ribs represent the dual life principles of the Maori, ira atua (the gods) and ira tangata (mankind), while the second suggests the ribs are a representation of the of the bill of the kotuku (white heron).

The other obvious feature found on most taurapa is the fairly naturalistic human figure which sits at the base. This figure is usually said to represent Puhi-kai-ariki, an ancestral god, and faces forward, overlooking the crew.

It is interesting to note that most of the surviving examples of taurapa show a remarkable consistency in design, which suggests there may be some long-held significance within the carving that was recognised pan-tribally.

## Waka Taua

Three beautifully carved taurapa from the Auckland Museum collection. The left and centre taurapa are from the Mair Collection, while the right hand taurapa is said to have belonged to Hongi Hika, and to have been abandoned at Pongakawa.
(AUCKLAND MUSEUM/TE PAPA WHAKAHIKU; LEFT TO RIGHT AM 144, AM 155 AND AM 267)

A striking feature of many taurapa was the feather ornamentation that was draped over them. These decorations usually consisted of two streamers of pigeon or kaka tail feathers trailing behind the waka, and a line of feathers across the top of the taurapa. Occasionally, as seen in the Parkinson engraving which dates from Cook's time in New Zealand (opposite), the fringe of feathers across the top of the taurapa extends right down its forward edge as well.

There was some variation in the naming conventions used for these feather decorations. One source states that puhi ariki, or puhi kai ariki, was the name given to the feathers that stretch across the top of the taurapa, and that the two streamers or tails of feathers were called puhi moana ariki. Another source uses the same names, but suggests that puhi kai ariki was the name of the streamer tied uppermost, while puhi moana ariki was the lower streamer. The term puhi rere was also used, but this seems to have been a general term applied to a pair of streamers trailing from a taurapa.

# Parts of the Waka

# Ra: Sails

It is believed that prior to the arrival of the European in New Zealand, ra, or sails, were a fairly common feature on waka taua. While only one example of an early Maori sail is known to have survived, and that is held in the British Museum, many early visitors to New Zealand recorded seeing waka with sails. It is probable that the introduction of easily obtainable and reasonably robust materials such as canvas and tarpaulin meant that labour-intensive sail-making quickly became outdated and was abandoned.

As well as the so-called British Museum sail, fine illustrations from a number of sources, including Abel Tasman's journal and later the works of artist G.F. Angas, have enabled ethnographers to reconstruct the design and rigging of early waka sails.

It seems that two distinct designs of sail were used, both triangular in shape and rigged with the apex down. The sails were generally constructed from either kiekie, harakeke (flax) or raupo, although Elsdon Best suggested that kutakuta was also used. Sails made from kiekie and harakeke were plaited in the same way as a mat would have been made. For their part, raupo leaves were

*A war canoe of New Zealand, with a view of Gable End Foreland, an engraving after a drawing by Sydney Parkinson. This fine illustration shows a large waka taua adorned with an impressive fringe of feathers across both the tauihu and the taurapa.*
(ALEXANDER TURNBULL LIBRARY, NATIONAL LIBRARY OF NEW ZEALAND/TE PUNA MATAURANGA O AOTEAROA, WELLINGTON)

## Waka Taua

*Taranaki or Mount Egmont. War canoe (early morning)*, by G.F. Angas. This painting of a waka taua under sail, dated 1847, features what was probably a raupo sail. It is interesting to note several of the crew paddling to hasten the canoe's progress. The crew would also have been charged with stabilising the waka in rough seas. (ALEXANDER TURNBULL LIBRARY, NATIONAL LIBRARY OF NEW ZEALAND/TE PUNA MATAURANGA O AOTEAROA, WELLINGTON)

laced together side by side, with the butt or wide end of the leaf uppermost, and the thinner ends converging at the sail's base. Two layers of raupo leaves were positioned one on top of the other, with two strings passed round each pair of leaves before the next pair was introduced. This lacing across the sail was repeated at intervals of five to eight cm down its length; the closer together the strings, the stronger the sail.

## RIGGING

It is believed that the sail was able to be rigged in two ways, either vertically or slanting. When rigged vertically, it was permanently fastened to the mast and sprit via loops plaited into each of its sides. The mast, typically made from tanekaha (celery pine), was lowered through a rope ring (takaore), which was lashed to the side of an adjacent taumanu, and the foot set in a mast shoe

# Parts of the Waka

carved into the floor of the hull. The mast was further supported by a rope on each side of the sail fastened to the taumanu holding the takaore, as well as by ropes to the front and rear. The sprit was attached to the mast by a loose rope ring, which allowed a certain amount of movement. Control of the sail was effected by means of a sheet tied to the sprit.

To lower the sail, it was first pulled in and, along with the sprit, securely lashed to the mast. Then, once the braces had been released, the mast was lifted from the takaore and lowered down the centre of the waka atop the taumanu.

Few details are known about the rigging of the slanting sail, other than that the sail was attached to both an upper yard and a lower boom, and that the short mast also rested in a mast shoe.

A mast being set in the takaore of a modern canoe from Anuta. While the mast of this canoe sits in the takaore, it is believed that the mast of a waka taua passed right through the rope ring and sat in a mast shoe carved into the hull of the canoe.

# Waka Taua

## THE BRITISH MUSEUM SAIL

The British Museum sail is described in the following text, edited and abridged, from a letter written in the late 1920s by J. Edge Partington.

*It is certainly a very old possession of the British Museum. I should think it is probably from the Cook collection, of which there is, I believe, nothing in the register beyond 'a collection presented by the Lords of the Admiralty'. I have no information about it.*

*From the excellence of the technique, and the fact that canoe-sails went out of use at so early a date after the coming of Europeans, it is clearly of great age, and may quite possibly have been secured by one of Cook's party. At all events it was almost certainly obtained by one of the early voyagers.*

*The dimensions of the sail are:*

| | |
|---|---|
| *Length:* | *14 ft 6 in.* |
| *Width at top:* | *6 ft 4 in.* |
| *Width at bottom:* | *1 ft.* |
| *Length of streamer:* | *3ft 6in.* |
| *Width of streamer:* | *9 in.* |

*It is made in 13 segments, running horizontally, each approximately 12 inches wide. There is a decorative pattern on the sail, of zigzag open-work. The zigzag lines run in pairs, one pair starting from the bottom and running medianly to the top, other pairs entering as the sail widens, until at the top there are five pairs of zigzags and the beginning of a sixth. The streamer is ornamented by 8 zigzags running vertically, also of open-work.*

*To the edges of the sail are fastened 24 loops, 12 on each edge, in the same plane as the sail itself. These are of multiple-strand flax cord, whipped with thin 2-strand cord. Each loop is*

# Parts of the Waka

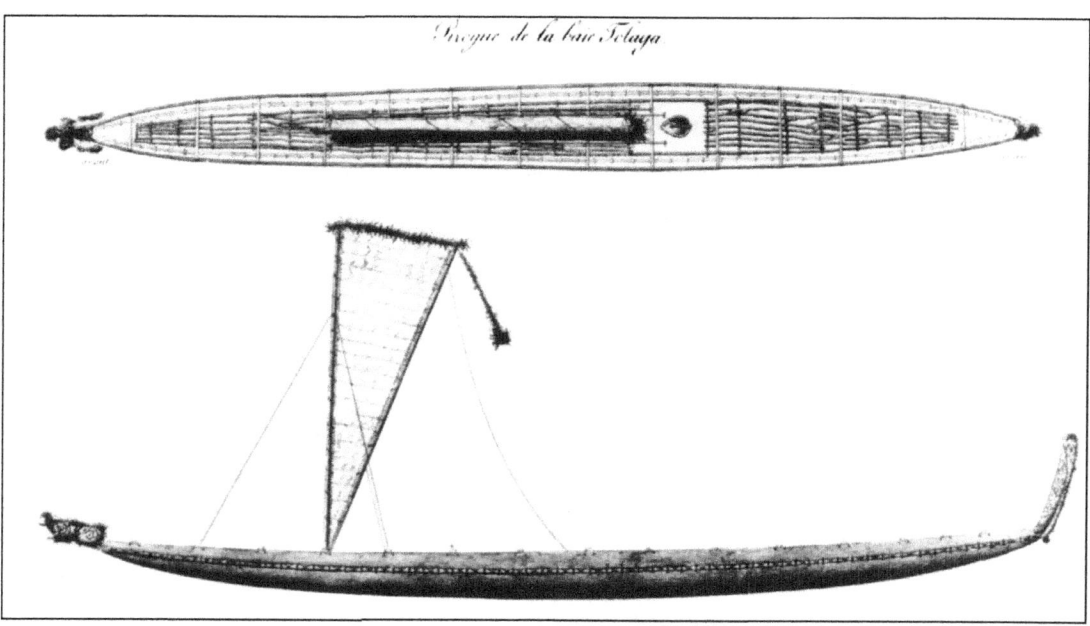

***Pirogue de la baie Tolaga.*** This illustration, from Jules Dumont d'Urville's ***Voyage de l'Astrolabe — Historique Partie 1***, shows a woven style of sail similar to that held by the British Museum. While the rigging is slightly different from that described by Edge Partington, the streamer and feather fringe are well illustrated, as are the horizontal panels of the sail.
(AUCKLAND MUSEUM/TE PAPA WHAKAHIKU)

approx. 4½ inches long and ³⁄₁₆–¼ inch thick. In many of the loops a little tuft of kaka feathers — red from the underwing — is fixed and held by the seizing cord. The technique of the loop-attachment is fairly simple. A running cord down the edge of the sail pierces it from the underside, comes round and through the eye of the loop, pierces the edge again, through the eye once more, and is bent behind to run on to the other loop-eye.

The body of the sail is made with a plain check-plait, the strips being fairly narrow, giving 10, 12, 13 or so to the inch. The streamer is made with the same technique. The edge of the sail is turned in, being folded in on itself twice. The resulting border appears in the underside of the sail and is ¾–1 inch wide. The lower edge of the sail has a serrated finish, displaying 6 triangles. As mentioned above, the technique of the body of the sail is plain check-plaiting. This is complicated, however, by the introduction of the zigzag openwork decorative design.

At the top of the sail are fixed tufts of feathers, in four sets, which are approximately ¾ inch apart. The feathers are fastened

## Waka Taua

*on in small tufts, the quills being bent over and tied to the shafts. The tufts are then secured by two running tie-cords about 1 inch apart, each of which is looped around each tuft and through the sail. Where the feathers are absent the serrated edge of the sail-top is seen. The feathers are apparently those of the hawk, but some may be those of the pigeon.*

*At the top left-hand corner of the sail (from a front view) the ends of the cord strengthening the top are braided up with the end of the edge cord running inside the lap.*

*A streamer is bound to the third strip of the sail from the top. It has a serrated edge along the top and bottom, with decorative feathers on all three free sides (top, bottom and end). The technique used to make the streamer is the same as that of [the] sail — i.e. plain check-plait, varied by zigzag openwork design for ornament, with about 10–12 strips to the inch. As with the sail, feather tufts are secured with a couple of turns of cord around the quill.*

## Punga: Anchors

Several types of punga, or anchor, were used for securing waka taua. Often an anchor was as simple as a woven basket full of rocks. Another fairly basic design was the equivalent of a modern grapnel anchor, consisting of three or four pieces of crooked timber (pohutukawa was a favourite) lashed together with a stone in the centre. When attached to a stout anchor rope, the arms of the anchor were designed to sink into the mud or shingle and there to hold fast.

Other anchors consisted of a single large rock formed roughly in the shape of a dumbbell, with a rope lashed tightly round the narrow middle. If a rock of the right shape could not be found,

# Parts of the Waka

Naturally shaped rocks, such as this one collected from the banks of the Whanganui River, were used as anchors whenever possible. Considerable effort would otherwise be required to drill a suitable hole for the anchor rope.

a groove would be made round the middle of an oval rock. Yet another style of anchor featured a hole drilled near the edge for the rope to pass through.

Punga which belonged to important waka or chiefs were often more elaborate. While similar in shape to the oval punga, they were sometimes incised with a pattern, usually of the rope, or spiral, style. These anchors would be named and well known.

Most ocean-going waka taua are believed to have carried an additional sea anchor. This was an open-ended woven basket in the shape of a windsock, which trapped water within its framework and acted as a heavy weight. The sea anchor would be lowered into the ocean from the bow end of the waka to a depth of approximately half the length of the vessel, and would keep the waka 'bow on' to any storm that might threaten it. To counterbalance the weight of the sea anchor after it had been lowered, the crew would move to the stern.

# Waka Taua

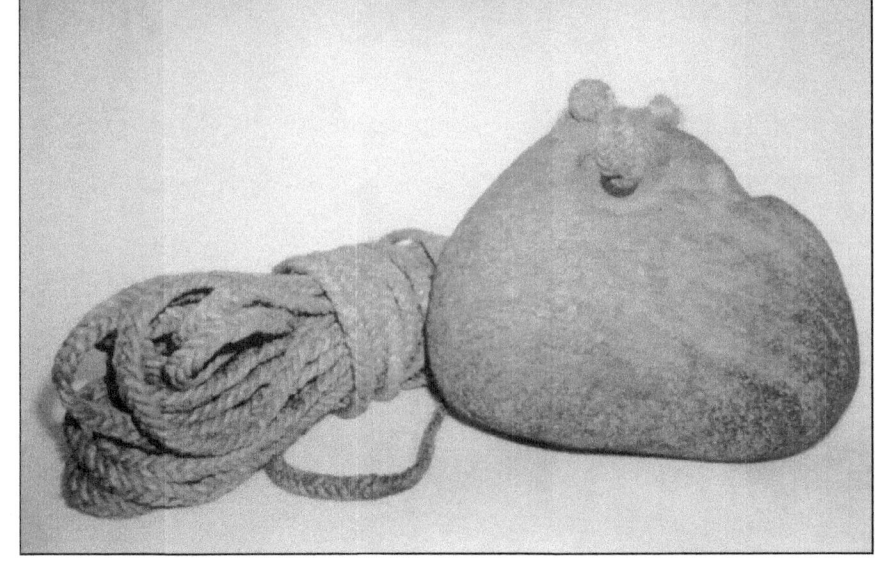

A typical example of an anchor stone, with a hole drilled for fastening the rope.
(AUCKLAND MUSEUM/TE PAPA WHAKAHIKU; AM 3147)

The following edited extract from Elsdon Best's *The Maori Canoe* describes how the crew pulled up the heavy anchor:

*A paddle is thrust, blade downwards, through the flooring, with its point behind one of the cross-pieces supporting the floor, and the upper and round part of the paddle resting on the gunwale and close against the thwart. Another paddle is laid horizontally across on the two gunwales and close against the other paddle. The rope cable is laid on this latter paddle, close against the slanting one, and the slack passed down the middle of the canoe. The rope runs in the angle made by the crossing of the handles of the two paddles, which, being jammed, prevent it sliding along the side of the canoe when hauled on. When the anchor was hauled up to the top board of the canoe, a stout pole was thrust through a loop of strong rope on the upper part of the anchor, then a number of men grasped the pole on either side of the anchor, and so lifted it in-board, where it was placed in the middle of the hold. The rope was then detached, and*

# Parts of the Waka

*coiled up carefully before re-attachment, so that when the anchor was again cast over, its rope would run free, without hitch or snarl.*

The anchor rope was just as important as the anchor itself. It was usually made by plaiting the unscraped leaves of the ti kauka tree in a four- or five-strand pattern, although sometimes vines from the climbing plant akakuku were used. It was customary to prepare the ti kauka leaves for plaiting by drying them in the shade, then leaving them submerged in water for some time. This made the leaves pliant and therefore easy to work with, and it also made them more durable.

## Tata: Bailers

Despite being working implements, tata (ta wai, tiheru) were often beautifully carved on the rim and handle, and those belonging to important waka were also often given names. Generally the design carved on the rim represented a human head. Tata were usually carved from a hard wood such as maire, matai or hinau.

Tata were of a perfect ergonomic design, carved with the handle turned inwards so that the man bailing could pivot his elbow on his thigh or knee and throw the water over the side of the waka behind him in one easy motion.

**This beautifully carved tata shows significant signs of use and age. The glossy patina on the handle attests to the extended use of the bailer, while the care taken in stitching the split confirms the bailer's value to its owner.**
(AUCKLAND MUSEUM/TE PAPA WHAKAHIKU)

# Waka Taua

**The Monck's Cave bailer is unique because to date it is the only bailer which has been found with the handle curving forward to join onto the side wall. It was discovered in a cave at Sumner, Christchurch, in 1889, along with an outrigger from a canoe and a painted paddle.**
(CANTERBURY MUSEUM/TE WHARE TAONGA-O-NGA-PAKIHI-WHAKATEKATEKA-O-WAITAHA; E 89.3.2)

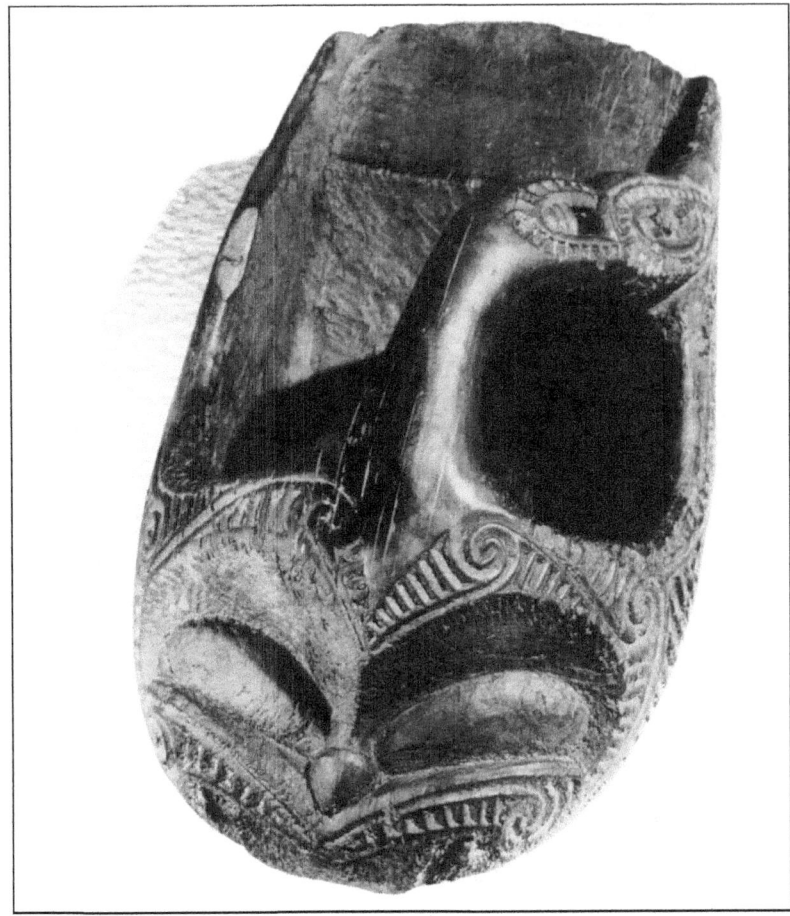

It is believed that karakia tata, or prayers, were sometimes chanted by those crew members charged with bailing as a waka was emptied. It is highly likely that a prayer such as the following, from Elsdon Best's *The Maori Canoe*, would have been used principally in particularly rough weather, as a plea for help to the gods:

*Mimiti pakora te tai tapu ki Hawaiki*
*Ararawa E! Kawea au ki uta*
*Te Kohu-tirikawa E! Kawea au ki uta*
*Ki te ahuru i uta, ki te tota i uta*
*Ki te moenga i uta*
*E au ai taku moe.*

# Paddling the Waka

## HOE: PADDLES

Waka taua were principally powered by paddles, or hoe — although, as mentioned, sails were also used when possible. Paddling hoe (as opposed to steering hoe) were generally between 140 and 170 cm long, and were usually made from either matai or manuka, both of these timbers being very light and strong. Maire or heart of pukatea were also suitable for paddle making. Although these paddles were finished with a thin blade, they were very strong and able to withstand the constant strain of paddling.

Unlike the longer steering paddles, which were perfectly straight from handle to blade, paddling hoe had their blade set forward at a slight angle from the handle. This ensured that the water was initially pushed down by the paddle and then pulled straight backwards, rather than the inefficient cycle of backwards and then up. Sometimes paddles had a slight scoop in the blade, which was said to help grip and hold the water, making paddling more efficient. Many paddles also had a small bump or knob at the tip of the blade, which was designed to stop the blade from splitting if it

## Waka Taua

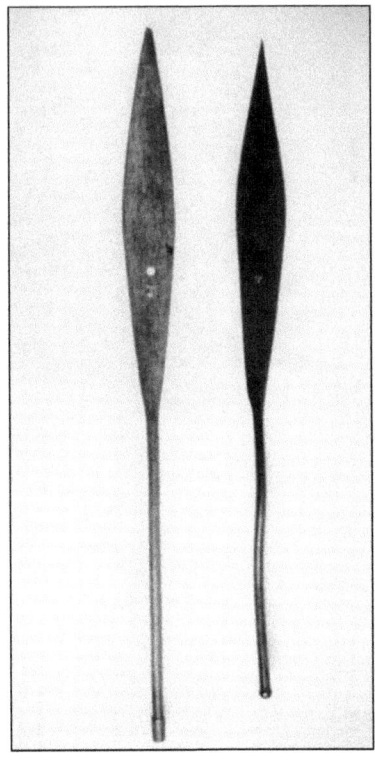

Different styles of hoe, or paddle. The paddle on the left is an example of the most common design, while the hoe with the curved handle is often described as a 'Waikato-style' paddle. (AUCKLAND MUSEUM/TE PAPA WHAKAHIKU)

was dropped or hit an underwater impediment such as a rock. Well-made paddles were said to balance exactly at the point where the handle and blade joined.

Although most paddle-makers followed a common basic design, a number of paddles differed from the norm. Paddles with curved handles (see illustration) are often referred to as Waikato style, although they are thought to have been produced in other regions as well. Another variation was the hoewai style of paddle, which was said to have been broad-bladed and designed to be used as a weapon when required.

### Decoration of paddles

Paddles were collected by a number of visitors to New Zealand, and they can be found in many museums and private collections around the world. The majority of those that survive have little or no carving on the blade, and no carving at all on the handle and top hand grip. The exceptions to this are paddles that were owned by chiefs, and those which were produced specifically for trading with Europeans.

Chiefs generally didn't paddle themselves, but used their paddle as a baton to encourage the crew or as a staff during ceremonies. These paddles were usually decorated with varying amounts of carving, painting, staining or, in some cases, charring. One such paddle is the spectacular whalebone paddle on display at Te Papa in Wellington, shown opposite, which is an incredible piece of craftsmanship.

The paddles that were produced for trade often had a kowhaiwhai pattern painted on one side and a figure carved on the other. They were a popular form of currency in the mid to later years of the nineteenth century.

# Paddling the Waka

Sydney Parkinson, who sailed to New Zealand with Cook, spoke of seeing in Poverty Bay 'paddles curiously stained with a red colour, disposed into various strange figures . . .', while George French Angas wrote of seeing charred paddles while at Taupo: 'In the canoes I have also observed several of the paddles elaborately ornamented with arabesque

designs in black and white, produced by charring the wood. Te Heuheu's son has been ornamenting some for me in a similar manner.'

It is interesting to note that although there is a lack of decoration on most paddling hoe collected in the North Island, a number of early South Island paddles had designs carved into the back of the blade, at the junction of the blade and the handle, or an extended ridge carrying on down the blade from the handle (see illustration, page 62). Because of their antiquity, it is difficult to ascertain whether these paddles were designed for everyday or ceremonial use. It should be noted that the carvings on them were generally in areas that would not be handled when the paddles were in use.

## Paddling Technique

It is not hard to imagine how physically demanding paddling would have been for the crew of a waka taua on a windless day.

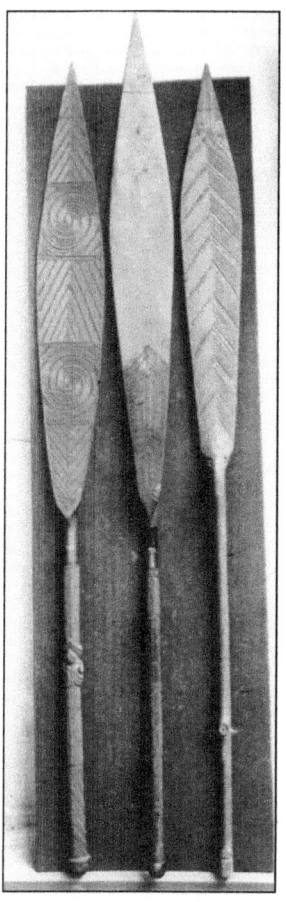

**These beautifully carved paddles were probably produced for trade rather than everyday use.**
(Auckland Museum/Te Papa Whakahiku)

**Above left: This very rare whalebone paddle, which features fine surface carving and back-to-back figures fashioned at the end of the handle, is currently on display at Te Papa in Wellington.**
(Auckland Museum/Te Papa Whakahiku)

## Waka Taua

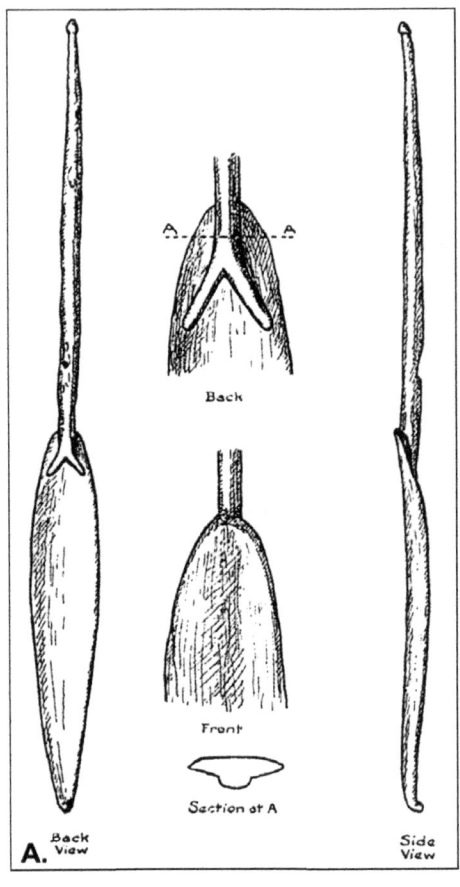

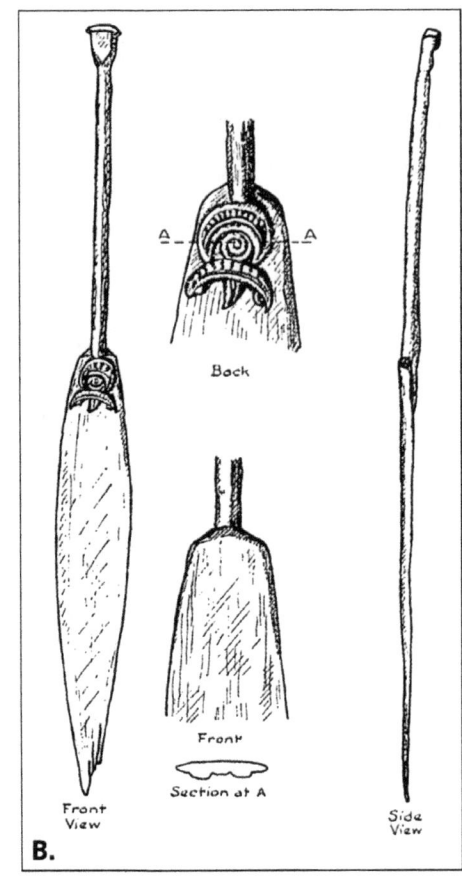

Two rare examples of early paddles from the South Island, now in the Otago Museum. The paddle shown in figure A was found in a cave at Bendigo, Central Otago, while that in figure B was found while digging a ditch on the shore of Lake Waihora. (JOURNAL OF THE POLYNESIAN SOCIETY)

The kaihoe, or paddlers, usually knelt, using their knees and lower back to wedge themselves between the taumanu.

Several different paddling techniques were used, and the kaihautu, or kai-tuki (time caller), would choose the most appropriate stroke depending on the conditions and the energy level of the crew.

When starting out, the crew first had to get the waka up to cruising, or planing, speed. This was accomplished by three deep, strong strokes, called whainene, followed by up to 40 sprint strokes, or pine. The whainene effectively pulled the waka from the water's grip, and the pine brought the vessel up to its optimum speed. When using the pine, only the bottom portion of the blade entered the water.

# Paddling the Waka

Once the waka taua was under way, the kai-hautu regularly varied the tempo of the paddling to ensure the desired speed was maintained, and that his paddlers were not worn out by long periods of sustained effort. The kai-hautu conveyed the required pace of the stroke by chanting or singing at different speeds.

If the kai-hautu wished to bring the waka up to full speed during a voyage, he would call for the deep, long houti stroke, at the same time as changing to a chant with a slightly slower beat. The houti stroke required the paddlers to give nearly 100 percent effort. It could not be maintained for long periods at a time, but was used in short bursts.

The following account, written by an early European resident of New Zealand, describes a fleet of waka racing out to a fishing ground. It highlights the use of paddling chants to regulate both the timing and the efforts of the crew.

> *Off we started to the refrain of 'Huka ka huka.' This is a light and rather quick stroke of the paddle, intended more to churn the water into foam rather than to gain speed . . . Then followed a most exciting race for the fishing-ground and the first fish. All through the fleet [of fifty canoes] the natives were shouting 'Hoea!' 'Tiaia!' 'Toia!' 'Pehia!' 'Ana kumea!' Roughly translated, these words are 'Pull!' 'Stick it in!' 'Drag it along!' 'Press it down!' 'Haul it along!' The last two mark deep, strong strokes of the paddles. The word ana is intended to make the stroke more strenuous; thus, at the words 'Ana toia!' 'Ana kumea!' &c., every ounce must be put into the stroke.*

J.L. Nicholas, another early visitor to New Zealand, also recorded his impressions of the regular, rhythmic mode of paddling employed by the Maori:

# Waka Taua

**Timing is all-important when paddling any craft, but especially when paddling waka taua. The concentration needed to keep in time shows on the faces of these kaihoe.**

*The New Zealanders have a custom, while paddling their canoes, to cheer and animate each other to exertion at stated intervals, by shouting out simultaneously certain words, and they regulate the movement of their paddles with regard to the depth of water in which they are to put them, and the rate the canoe is to proceed at, whether fast or slow, by each of these words. All this is done with such methodical exactness, and such wonderful unison of the paddles that it would be supposed there was but one soul to give impulse to the whole of them.*

For periods when sustained speed was required over longer distances, the kai-hautu often called for the ha stroke, or alternate light and strong strokes. This allowed the paddler to give a full effort every second stroke, and recover in between with a stroke requiring perhaps 50 percent power. The beauty of the intermittent light stroke was that not only did the paddler get a rest, which helped extend his paddling range, but it also ensured that the

# Paddling the Waka

waka's speed was maintained, as described in the following quote from T.H. Pott's book, *Out in the Open*:

> *Each plunge of the paddles is directed by the kai-hautu, who shakes his paddle, or quivers his fingers, in exact time with the chant with which he encourages the rowers. Time is kept with most wonderful precision; the thirty paddles in the canoe dash aside the water at the same instant. The stroke most frequently used is one strong plunge of the paddle, which is succeeded by a mere dip, which lasts while the way is on the canoe given by the preceding strong stroke.*

A stroke often employed during rough weather was the hahama. This was a light, fast stroke, for which only the bottom of the blade was submerged. The hahama was particularly useful in choppy water, where use of a full blade might cause difficulties.

The ability of the crew to time their paddling with such precision was often a source of wonder to early visitors to these shores. Recording sentiments that were commonly expressed, Joseph Banks remarked in his journal:

> *I have seen fifteen paddles of a side in one of their canoes move with immensely quick strokes, and at the same time as much justness as if the rowers were animated by one soul; not the fraction of a second could be observed between the dipping and raising of any two of them, the canoe all the while moving with incredible swiftness . . . So much strength, firmness, and agility did they show in their motions, and at the same time such excellent time did they keep, that I have often heard above a hundred paddles struck against the sides of their boats, as directed by their singing, without a mistake being ever made.*

# Waka Taua

*In managing these canoes — at least, in paddling them — they are very expert. In one I counted sixteen paddles on a side, and never did men, I believe, keep better time with their strokes, driving on the boat with immense velocity.*

The crew also needed to be skilled in more than basic paddling. One observer described how, when a waka began to list dangerously in rough water, paddlers on the side the swell was coming from leant out over the rauawa and 'thrust their paddles deep into the wave, and by a curious action force[d] the water under the canoe', thus correcting the waka. On another occasion, an early eyewitness, watching as a waka arrived at the bar of a rivermouth, saw the crew jump overboard and, holding the sides of their vessel, balance her as they rode through the swell.

## STEERING PADDLES

Steering paddles (hoe peperu or hoe urungi) were generally between 1.8 and 2.7 m long, and differed from common paddles in having a straight profile, rather than the slightly angled blade used for paddling. They were traditionally made from heavy woods like maire and matai, which could withstand the immense pressure exerted during turning, and their handles were often carved in the shape of a manaia.

Seated at the base of the taurapa, the kaiwhakatere, or steersman, used his steering paddle to keep the waka on course and out of trouble. It took a lot of skill to steer such a low-sided vessel, especially in heavy seas or fast rivers. Despite the increased freeboard afforded by the rauawa, and the occasional use of a plaited mat to cover the front metres of a waka's hold, it was not uncommon for even large waka to be swamped. In particularly rough

# Paddling the Waka

A kaiwhakatere, or steersman, skilfully guiding his waka along the Waikato River.

weather, water would break over the rauawa and fill the hull as fast as the crew could bail. To capsize in these conditions could spell disaster for the crew.

It was the steersman's responsibility to keep the waka safe at all times, and an experienced crew reacted to his instructions instantly and without question. In an emergency, crew members sitting near the back of the waka might be called upon to assist the steersman.

In large waka it was common to have a second steersman positioned at the bow, whose job it was to watch for instances of oversteering and adjust the waka's course accordingly. He was able to do this by thrusting his paddle deep into the water on the appropriate side, and turning the blade at an oblique angle.

## Waka Taua

# KAI-HAUTU: THE TIME CALLER

As described earlier, the role of the kai-hautu (or kai-tuki) was to regulate the tempo of the paddlers' strokes. As he strode up and down the waka along the taumanu he often displayed an almost uncanny sense of balance. The following account was recorded by Dr Ferdinand von Hochstetter after he had witnessed a waka taua at full speed.

> *The kai-tuki, by singing and various gesticulations, incites the crew to ply their paddles, and denotes, by the rhythm of the song he chooses, the greater or less rapidity of stroke desired. Such a song is called tuki-waka. In large war-canoes, manned sometimes by sixty or seventy men, there are generally two kai-tuki acting as leaders, one placed near the bow and the other the stern. In addition to their voices, they have in the hand some native weapon which they brandish in time. They either sing by turns, one responding to the other; or they sing together, extemporising at the same time various jokes and witticisms, by introducing into the traditional songs new verses having reference to the momentary situation. It is remarkable to see how the pullers are in this manner guided in keeping time. With as regular strokes as if managed by one hand, the paddles are moving on both sides, and with the same regularity the bodies of all the pullers are moving now forward, now backward; and as the time increases in velocity these motions also become faster and more energetic, until at last, with an almost convulsive tossing forward and backward of the head and the whole upper part of the body, their hair streaming in the air, the whole crew in wild chorus is repeating the last syllables or words of each verse chanted by the leaders. The sight of such a war-canoe manned and decked with festal drapery, while, propelled by the simultaneous strokes*

# Paddling the Waka

*of sixty or more paddles, it darts along almost with the velocity of a steamboat, produces an imposing but almost an uncomfortably savage impression. It has the appearance of one body with a hundred arms and as many feet, every part of which is alive and in motion, like a gigantic centipede upon the water.*

The effort-inspiring chants were not used constantly, but called when extra power and speed were required. It would have been physically impossible for the paddlers to continue at maximum effort indefinitely.

When not chanting, the key role of the kai-hautu was to concentrate on the feel of the waka's progress, and to adjust the crew's strokes as required. If he felt the waka was a little sluggish in the water, he might ask for more effort. If on the other hand the men had been paddling hard for a prolonged period, he might order a change from the houti stroke to the ha stroke. To mark any change in effort, the vowels of the kai-hautu's chant were lengthened or shortened in accordance with the time the paddles spent in the water.

**Charged with the overall responsibility for his waka, the kai-hautu must also urge his kaihoe on when their muscles are burning and their lungs are screaming out for a rest.**

# Appendix: Paddling Instructions

The following are paddling instructions for kaihoe of the waka taua *Ngatokimatawhaorua*. They have been provided by Robin Reed, a waka taua veteran from the Bay of Islands.

| Kai-hautu | Kaihoe | Action and translation |
|---|---|---|
| **To get ready:** | | |
| Tukua. | | Sit relaxed with the hoe inboard. |
| Nga hoe rite. | | Sit with your hoe ready to paddle. |
| | | |
| **The salute:** | | |
| | | Ready the canoe. |
| Te waka kia rite! | Hi! Ha! | Hoe go up to the vertical on 'Ha!' |
| | | The same command is used to return to the ready-to-paddle position. |
| | | |
| **To go forwards:** | | |
| Te ihu kia rite? | | Is the bow (nose) ready? |
| Waenga kia rite? | | Is the middle ready? |
| Te kei kia rite? | | Is the stern ready? |
| Te waka ki mua! | | The waka goes forwards! |
| Tena whakataua. | | This waka and crew. |
| | Anana koia hoki! | Let it be so, we are ready! |
| Rite kia rite. | | Commence paddling. |
| | Tokihi tokihi! | We are paddling. |
| | | |
| **To paddle rapidly:** | | |
| Tuara piko ana. | | Reach fully forward and take a full blade with rapid power strokes. |
| | | |
| Rite kia rite. | | Commence rapid paddling. |

# Appendix

| Kai-hautu | Kaihoe | Action and translation |
|---|---|---|
| <u>To return to normal paddling:</u> | | |
| Te waka patu kau. | | The paddlers concerned return to normal forward paddling. |
| Rite kia rite. | | Commence action. |
| <u>To go backwards:</u> | | |
| Te waka ki muri! | | The waka goes backwards! Paddlers reverse their paddles ready to paddle backwards. |
| Rite kia rite. | | Commence paddling backwards. |
| <u>Turning the waka:</u> | | |
| Huakina. | | Reach straight out to the side of the waka and pull the water inwards to the side of the waka. |
| Tupoua. | | Dig into the water beside the waka hull and push out. <br> OR (when the waka is under way) <br> Place your hoe straight down beside the waka hull, blade facing forward at about 30 degrees, and hold it steady. |
| <u>The salute on the move:</u> | | |
| Ka nuku nuku. | Ka neke neke. | Move up, move gently. |
| Ka nuku nuku. | Ka neke neke. | Move up, move gently. |
| | *Ngatokimatawhaorua* tenei. | This is the waka *Ngatokimatawhaorua*. |
| | E hora nei. | Before you. |
| | Au Au Aue hi! | |
| | Ha! | Paddles go up to vertical salute position. |
| Te waka kia rite! | Hi!   Ha! | Paddles go down to paddling position, and paddling recommences on 'Ha!' |

# Glossary

| | |
|---|---|
| **Ha** | Paddling technique that alternates light and strong strokes. |
| **Hahama** | Light, fast stroke using only the tip of the paddle. |
| **Hapu** | Sub-tribe, clan. |
| **Haumi kokomo** | An addition to the hull attached to either end of the waka with a mortice and tenon joint. |
| **Hihi** | Plumed rods projecting from the tauihu (usually called ihiihi). |
| **Hoe** | Paddle. |
| **Hoe peperu** | Steering paddle. |
| **Hoe urungi** | Steering paddle. |
| **Hoewai** | Broad-bladed paddle also used as a weapon. |
| **Houti** | Deep, long paddling stroke. |
| **Huaki** | Carved figure on the rear of the splashboard looking into the waka. |
| **Hune** | Pappus of the seeds of the raupo plant. |
| **Ihiihi** | Plumed rods projecting from the tauihu (also called hihi). |
| **Ira atua** | Life principle of gods and supernatural beings. |
| **Ira tangata** | Life principle of human beings. |
| **Kaea** | Song or chant caller. |
| **Kaha** | Lashing cord. |
| **Kai-hautu (-tuki)** | Captain of a waka, and usually the time caller for paddling. |
| **Kaihoe** | Paddler. |
| **Kaiwhakatere** | Steersman. |
| **Karakia tata** | Incantation chanted while bailing. |
| **Karamea** | A clay used in painting or staining the waka. |
| **Karu atua** | The hoops on the end of the ihiihi; literally 'eye of god'. |
| **Kawa** | Ceremony to free the waka of tapu and ready it for everyday use. |
| **Kokowai** | Red ochre. |

# Glossary

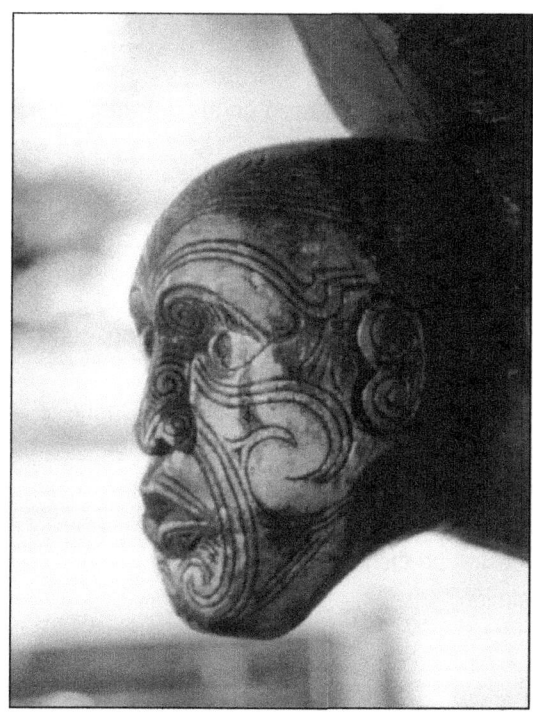

Parata on the waka taua *Te Ika a Maui*.

| | |
|---|---|
| **Koneke** | Carving sometimes present on the hull under the tauihu. |
| **Kotahitanga** | Unification. |
| **Kowhaiwhai** | Scroll pattern in carving or painting. |
| **Kowhao** | Lashing hole. |
| | |
| **Manaia** | Stylised, beaked figure common in Maori carving. |
| **Matiti** | Small wooden wedge. |
| **Maunga taura** | Bulkhead. |
| **Mimiro** | Y-shaped tool used for pulling lashing cord tight (also called tanekaha). |
| | |
| **Neke** | Skid or roller. |
| **Ngaro** | Skid or roller. |
| **Ngatoa** | Style of scalloped finish on the outside of the hull. |
| **Niao** | Top edge of the hull proper. |
| **Noa** | Free from tapu. |
| | |
| **Pa** | Fortified village. |
| **Paiwai** | Inner batten covering the join between the rauawa and the hull. |
| **Parapara** | Sediment. |
| **Parata** | Carved head sometimes lashed to the front of the hull. |

# Waka Taua

| | |
|---|---|
| **Pare-ngarungaru** | Scalloped finish sometimes used on the outside of waka hulls. |
| **Pia houhou** | Tacky gum used as a caulking agent. |
| **Pine** | Sprint strokes used in paddling. |
| **Pitau** | Carved spirals; carved prow of a waka taua. |
| **Pounamu** | Greenstone. |
| **Puhi-kai-ariki** | Both the figure facing into the hull of the taurapa, and the top feather decoration on the taurapa. |
| **Puhi moana ariki** | Generic name for the two streamers attached to the taurapa. |
| **Puhi rere** | Alternative name for the two streamers attached to the taurapa. |
| **Puhoro** | Painted design on the hull under the tauihu. |
| **Puna-wai** | Bailing station. |
| **Punga** | Anchor. |
| **Putiki** | Bulkhead. |
| **Ra** | Sail. |
| **Rahoraho** | Waka flooring. |
| **Rangi waka** | Canoe-hauling song. |
| **Rango** | Skid or roller. |
| **Rape** | Spiral. |
| **Rauawa** | Topstrake or gunwale. |
| **Raura** | Five-stranded rope. |
| **Ta wai** | Bailer. |
| **Taingawai** | Bailing station. |
| **Taioma** | Pipeclay. |
| **Taka** | Batten covering the join between the rauawa and the hull. |
| **Takaore** | Rope ring that houses the mast. |
| **Tanekaha** | Y-shaped tool used for pulling lashing cord tight (also called mimiro). |
| **Tane Mahuta** | Guardian of the forest. |
| **Tangaroa** | Guardian of the ocean. |
| **Tangata whenua** | Local inhabitant(s); people of the land. |
| **Tapu** | Under religious or superstitious restriction. |
| **Tata** | Bailer. |
| **Tauihu** | Prow of a waka. |

# Glossary

| | |
|---|---|
| **Taumanu** | Thwart. |
| **Taurapa** | Stern-piece of a waka. |
| **Tawharau** | Canoe shed. |
| **Te Wao-nui-o-Tane** | Domain of Tane Mahuta; the forest. |
| **Tiheru** | Bailer. |
| **Tohunga tarai waka** | Master canoe builder. |
| **Toiere** | Carving sometimes present on the hull under the tauihu. |
| **Toki tarai waka** | Stone adze used for making waka. |
| **Toki umarua** | Double-shouldered adze. |
| **Tuere** | Carved prow of a waka taua, commonly referred to as 'northern style'. |
| **Tuki-waka** | Song or chant of the time caller. |
| **Waka** | Canoe. |
| **Waka huhunu (hunua, unua)** | Permanent double canoe. |
| **Waka taua** | War canoe. |
| **Waka taurua** | Temporary double canoe. |
| **Ware houhou** | Tacky gum used as a caulking agent. |
| **Whainene** | Deep, strong paddling strokes. |
| **Whakainu waka** | Waka launching. |
| **Whakanoa** | Free from tapu. |
| **Wharau** | Canoe shed. |
| **Whare wananga** | School of higher learning. |

# Recommended Reading

Elsdon Best, *The Maori Canoe*. Government Printer, Wellington, 1976.

Sir Peter Buck, *The Coming of the Maori*. Whitcoulls, Wellington, 1987.

A.C. Haddon and James Hornell, *Canoes of Oceania*. Bishop Museum Press, Honolulu, 1991.

Anne Nelson, *Nga Waka Maori*. Macmillan, Auckland, 1991